Content:

1. What is Crowdfunding & Fundraising

2. List of Crowdfunding Websites

3. How to Create Campaign at Gofundme

4. How to Create Campaign at Kickstarter

5. How to Create Campaign at Uphatter

6. How to Create Campaign at Indiegogo

7. How to Create Campaign at any Crowdfunding or Fundraising Websites

8. How to Promote Crowdfunding or Fundraising Campaign

1. What is Crowdfunding & Fundraising

Crowdfunding is a way to raise money for an individual or organization by collecting donations through family, friends, friends of friends, strangers, businesses, and more. There are three types of crowdfunding donation-based, rewards-based, and equity crowdfunding.

- Donation-Based Crowdfunding

Broadly speaking, it's correct to think of any crowdfunding campaign in which there is no financial return to the investors or contributors as donation-based crowdfunding.

Common donation-based crowdfunding initiatives include fundraising for disaster relief, charities, nonprofits, and medical bills.

- **Rewards-Based Crowdfunding**

Rewards-based crowdfunding involves individuals contributing to a business in exchange for a "reward," typically a form of the product or service the company offers.

Even though this method offers backers a reward, it's still generally considered a subset of donation-based crowdfunding since there is no financial or equity return.

- **Equity-Based Crowdfunding**

Unlike the donation-based and rewards-based methods, equity-based crowdfunding allows contributors to become part-owners of a company by trading capital for equity shares. As equity owners, contributors receive a financial return on their investment and ultimately receive a share of

the profits in the form of a dividend or distribution.

2. List of Crowdfunding Websites

There are hundreds of crowdfunding websites but we listed only trusted companies.

- Gofundme
- Kickstarter
- Uphatter
- Indiegogo
- Fundly
- Facebook

3. How to Create Campaign at Gofundme

To create you need to signup at Gofundme and create an account.

Click at Start Campaign, it will redirect to signup page. Now create account

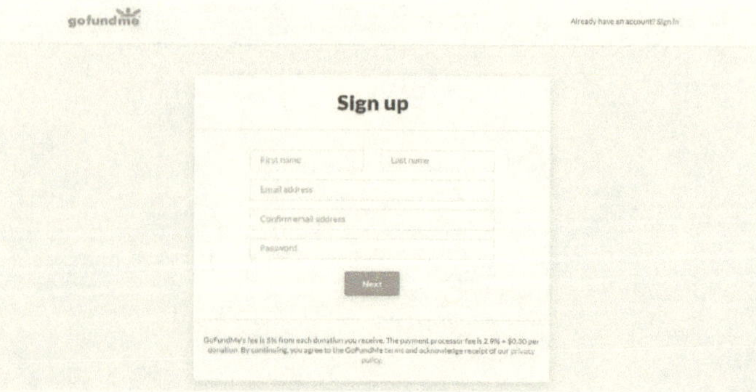

After login, click at create campaign, it will redirect you to below page. Ath this page, you need to insert title, description, images and goal.

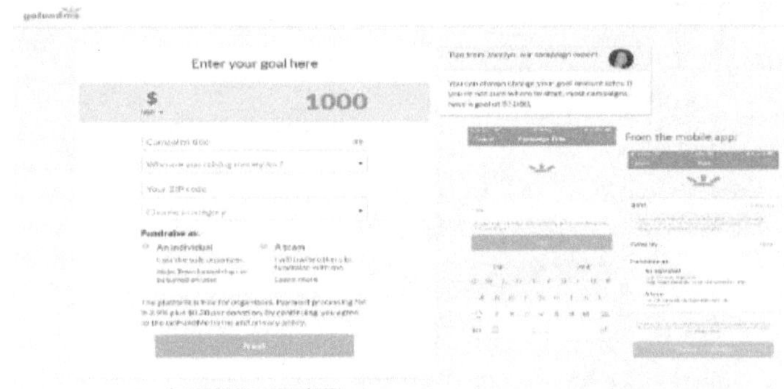

That's it, your campaign will be published at Gofundme immediately and will look like, you can raise funds for any cause, business and project with Gofundme.

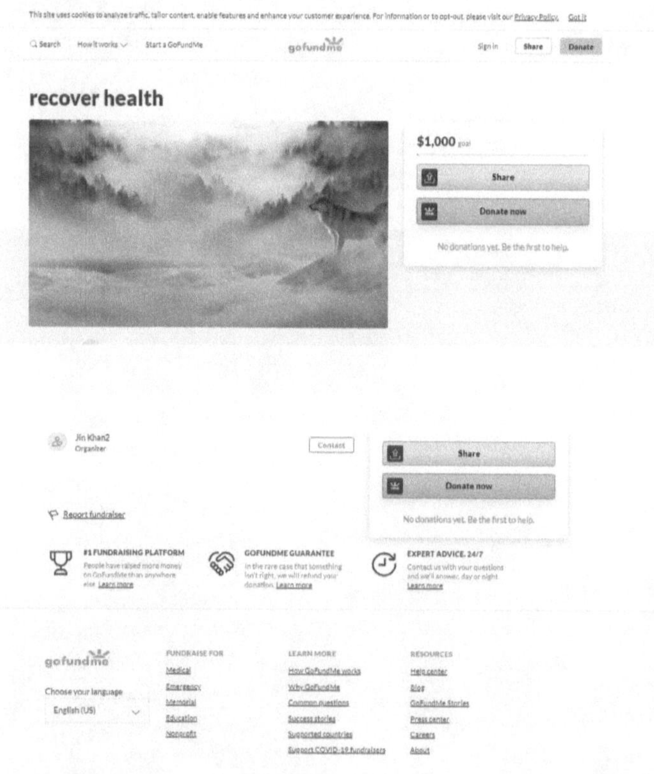

4. How to Create Campaign at Kickstarter

To create campaign at Kickstart, you need to have Kickstarter account. You can signup

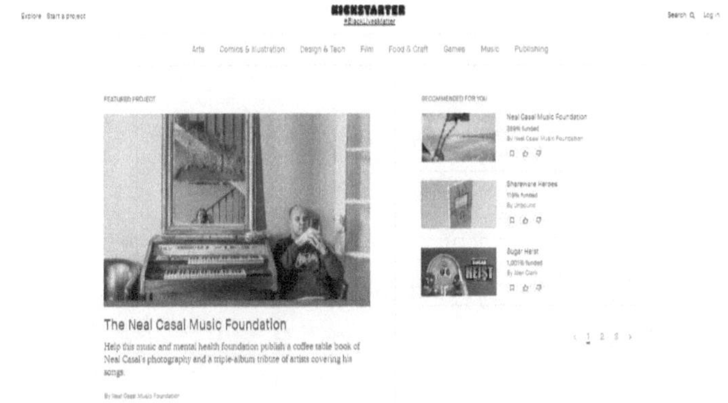

Now click at Start a project at top left side. Press it and it will take you at signup page

After login click at start project and choice category, provide campaign title, country name

1. Choose a category:

   Select a category ⌄

2. Give your project a title:

   title...

3. Your permanent residence:

   Select your country ⌄

Now add image, project title, short blurb

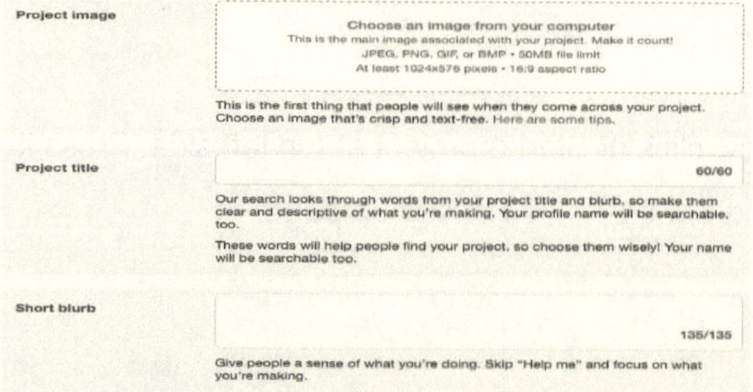

Now set rewards, add title, pledge amount, description, select delivery date and submit

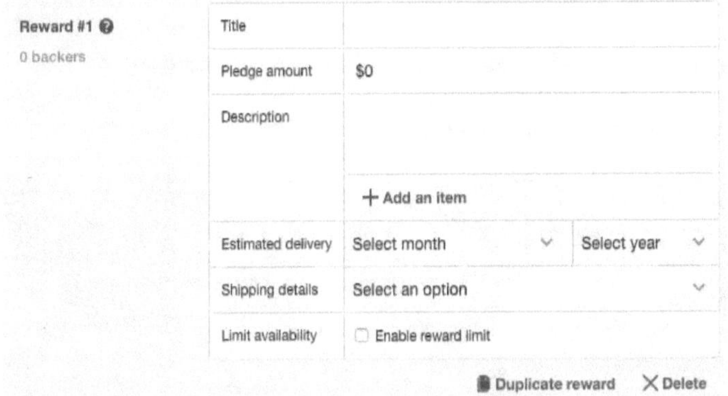

That's it, now your campaign will be live within few minutes

Now add you biography

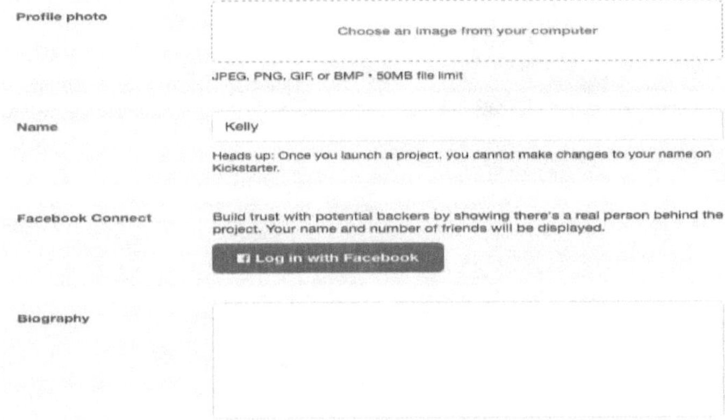

5. How to Create Campaign at Uphatter

To create campaign at Uphatter, you need to signup or have account.

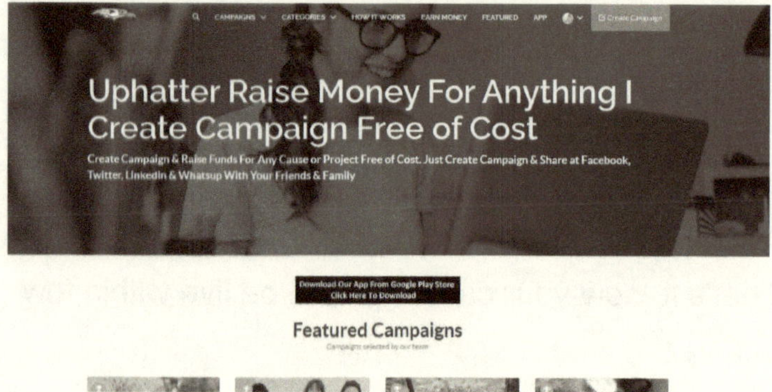

Once you signup, please at campaign button, it will redirect you to below page

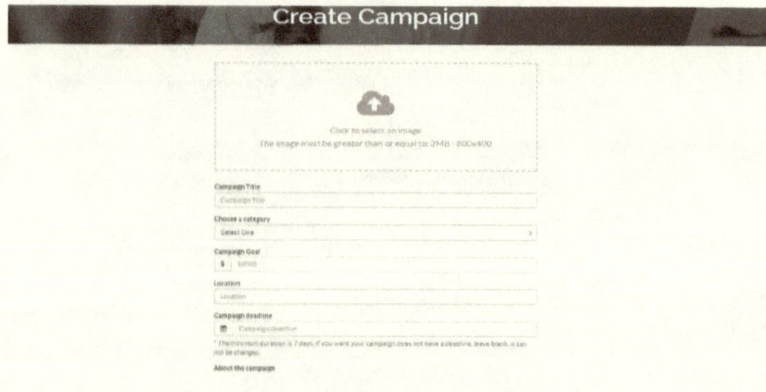

Now insert image, title, select category, enter campaign goal, location and description and press at submit button.

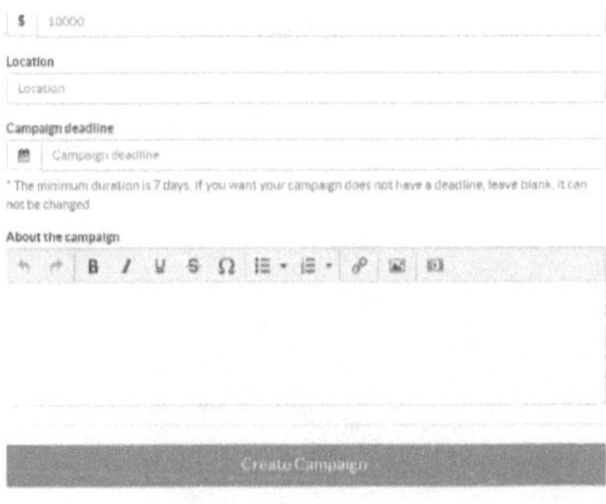

Your campaign will be live within few seconds and will look like

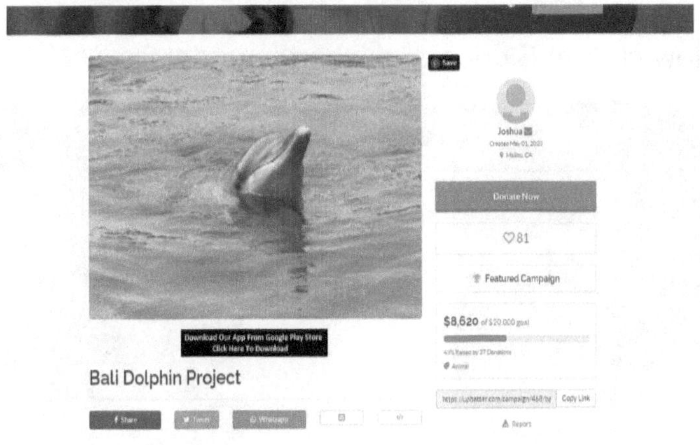

6. How to Create Campaign at Indiegogo

To create campaign at Indiegogo, you need to have account, if you don't have you can signup

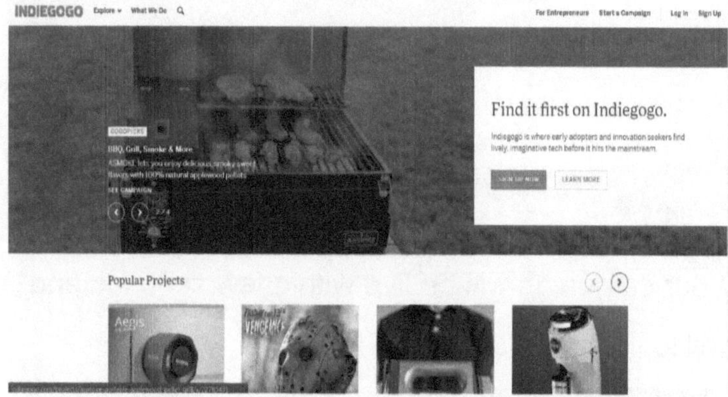

Now click at Signup and insert your details.

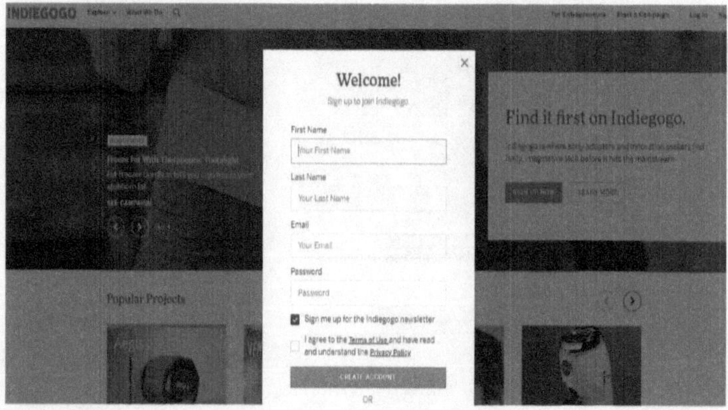

After login, click at create campaign, it will redirect to below page.

Now select indiegogo and it will take you to below page. Select your country and insert bank details and press start campaign

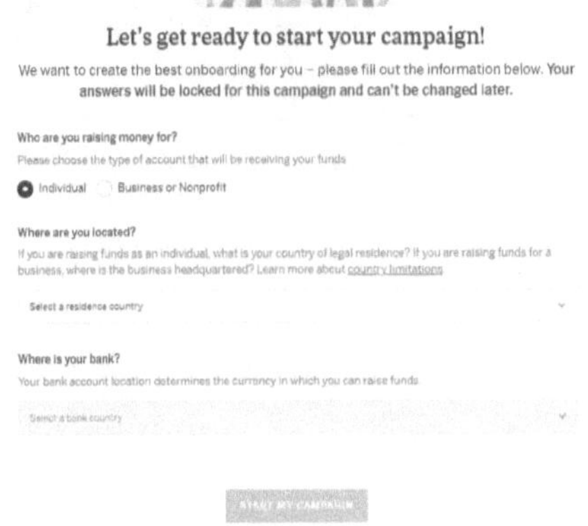

Now select basic from sidebar and insert campaign title, tagline, upload image, select location, select category, insert tags, insert campaign duration and press save and continue button

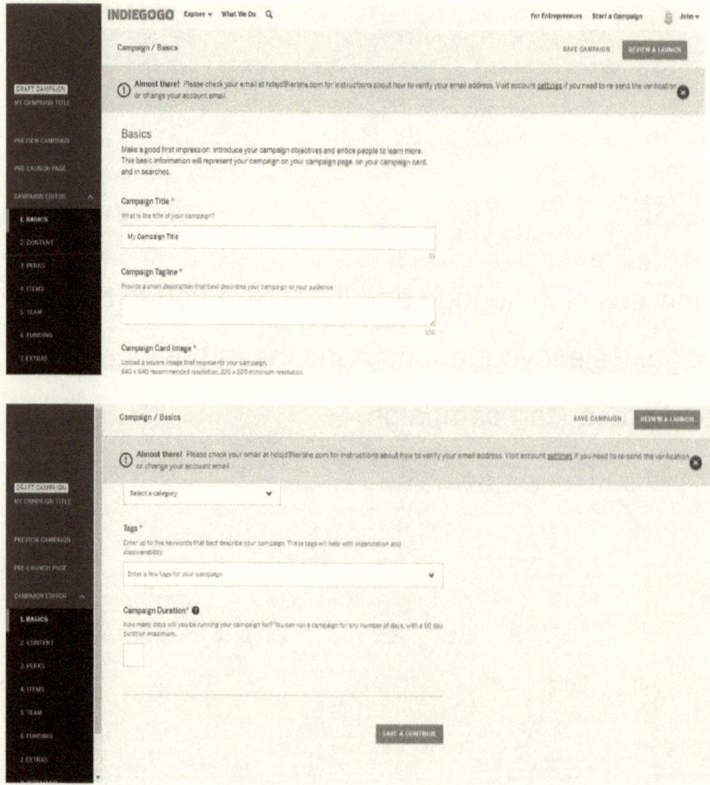

Now select content from sidebar and insert video or image, story, insert questions and answers and press save & continue button

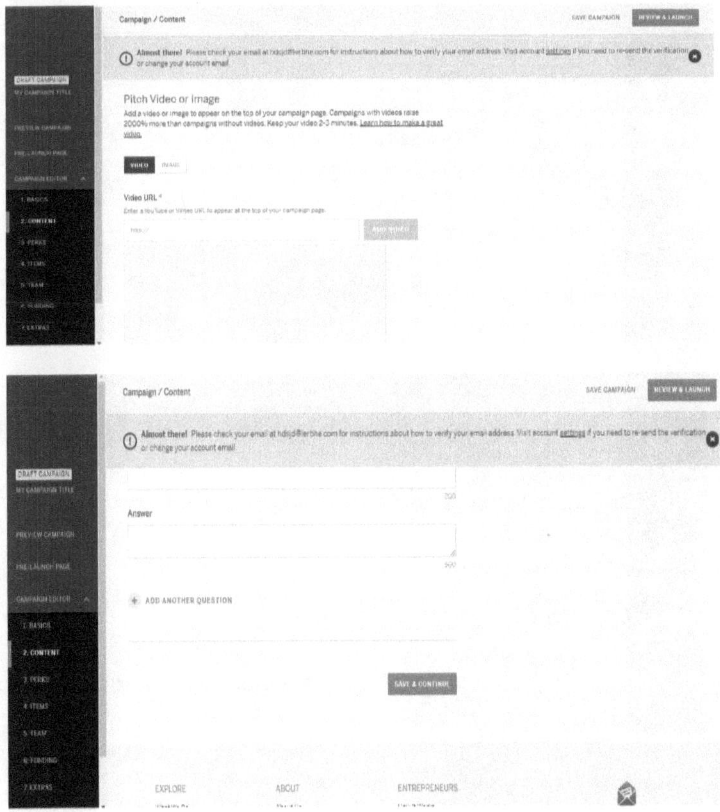

Now select plerk from sidebar and insert details, after that press save button

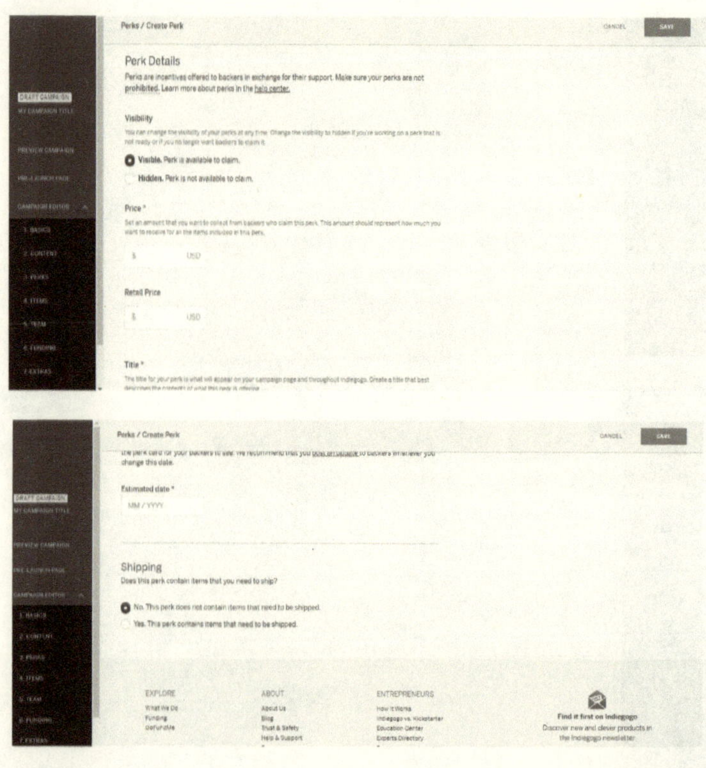

Now select team from sidebar and insert details as shown in below images and press review and launch button.

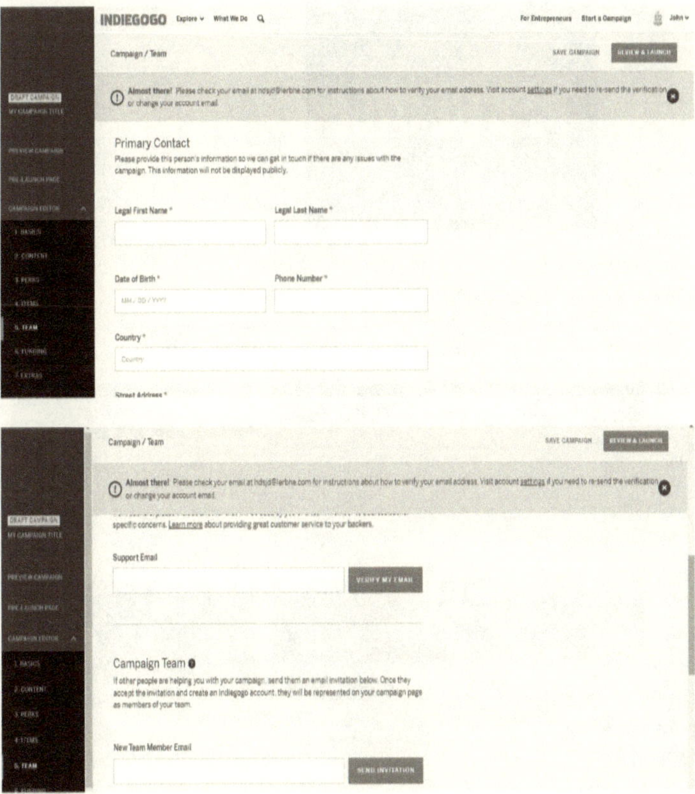

Your campaign will immediately published at Indiegogo and will look like.

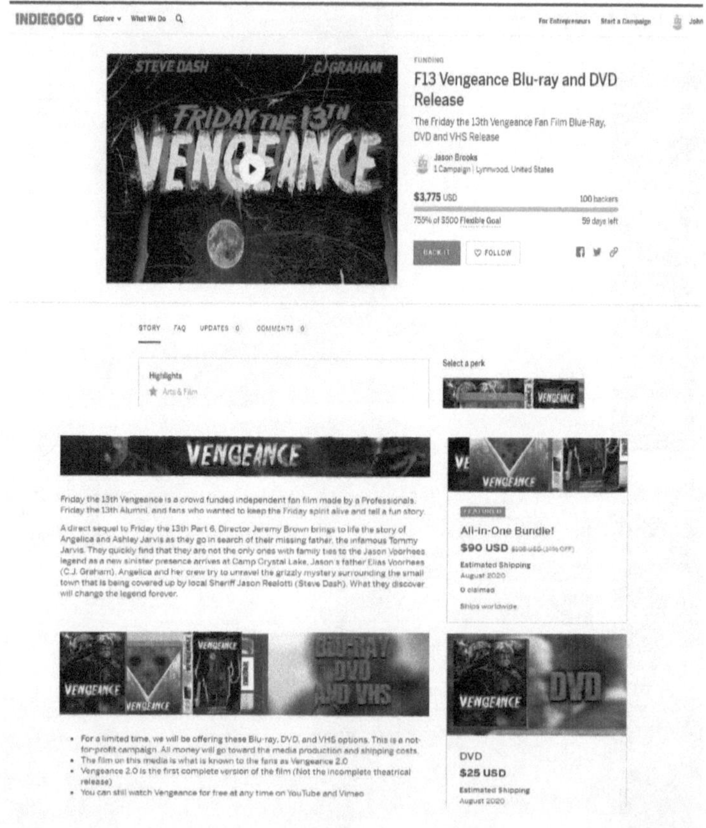

7. How to Create Campaign at any Crowdfunding or Fundraising Websites

As we mentioned there are hundreds of crowdfunding and fundraising sites at internet. But researched about it and only mentioned trusted websites. If you also want to list your campaign at other websites, it's good the process is same, you need to signup and then create campaign. Also its a good trick whenever you are ready to launch campaign, list it at every crowdfunding & fundraising websites. By using this trick, your campaign goal will be fulfilled soon.

8. How to Promote Crowdfunding or Fundraising Campaign

It is the most important part to increase chances for the success of your campaign. Please follow below instructions

- **Share your campaign**

After creating campaign, share it at your own social media account like Facebook, Twitter, Linkedin, Whatsup etc. Its a free marketing strategy

- Facebook Advertising

You can promote you campaign with Facebook paid marketing.

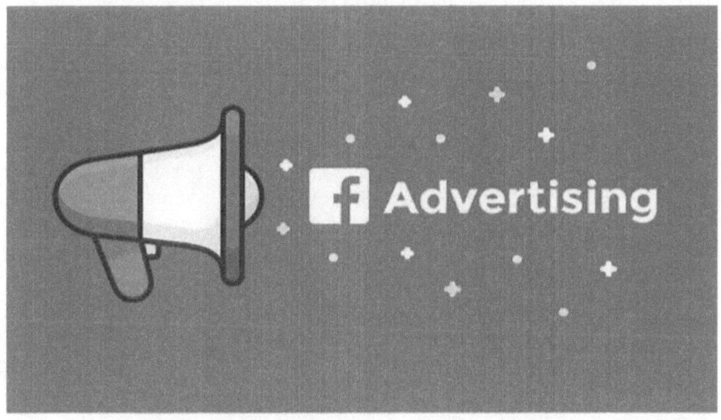

- Email Marketing

If you have list of emails, you can send your campaign to them. Its a good free marketing tool.

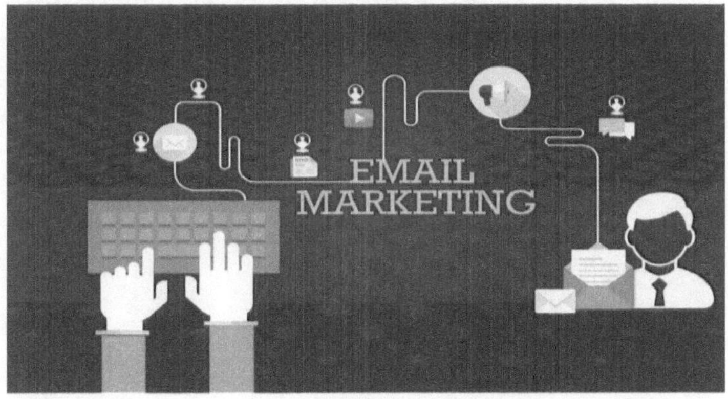

- Social Media Influencer

Contact social media influencers who have millions of followers. They will charge some amount and can share your campaign link infront of there followers, it's also a good marketing tool to reach your campaign goal

- Facebook Groups

Join crowdfunding or fundraising related groups at Facebook and share your campaign link. Its a free marketing strategy

- Live Streams

You can also use live streaming on platforms like Kickstarter to build a relationship with your existing followers and gain new ones.

- In-Person Events

In-person events are another way that you can generate leads and get more backers for your crowdfunding campaign

- **Crowdfunding Forum**

Crowdfunding Forum is another resource that we've put together to help you with your campaign. You can use it to connect with other entrepreneurs. You can also share your project with crowdfunding enthusiasts.

- **Referral Programs**

More and more, I've seen crowdfunders use Indiegogo's referral tool to incentivize influencers to share their project. A referral program is a great way to set up a win-win situation where you'll get more traffic and they'll be rewarded for their efforts.

- **Reddit**

There are many communities on reddit that function as online forums where you can discuss topics or share your project.

- **Podcasts**

Lastly, there are a growing number of podcasts on iTunes that you can tap into to share your story.

That's it. Please follow each marketing steps to reach your campaign goal soon.

If you have any question, please feel free to contact me. Thank you

Have a Great Day!